✦ SECRETS OF THE RAINFOREST ✦

RESOURCES AND CONSERVATION

BY MICHAEL CHINERY

🌳 CRABTREE

Crabtree Publishing Company

PMB 16A, 350 Fifth Avenue Suite 3308
New York, NY 10118

612 Welland Avenue St. Catharines, Ontario
Canada L2M 5V6

Created by Cherrytree Press
© Evans Brothers Limited 2001

Library of Congress Cataloging-in-Publication Data

Chinery, Michael.
    Resources and conservation / by Michael Chinery.
        p. cm.– (Secrets of the rainforest)
    ISBN 0-7787-0221-9 (RLB) – ISBN 0-7787-0231-6 (pbk.)
    1. Rain forests. 2. Rain forest conservation. 3. Rain forest ecology. I. Title.

SD247 .C45 2001   LC 00-060389
333.75'16'0913–dc21   CIP

Co-ordinating Editor: Ellen Rodger
Copy Editor: Lisa Gurusinghe
Proofreader: Mary-Anne Luzba
Designed and produced by A S Publishing
Editor: Angela Sheehan
Design: Richard Rowan
Artwork: Malcolm Porter
Consultant: Sue Fogden

Acknowledgements
Photographs: *BBC Natural History Unit* Cover, 4, 5 center, 6, 6/7,
7 top, 8, 8/9, 9 bottom left, 10 top, 10 bottom, 11 top center
& bottom, 12 top, 13 bottom right, 14/15 top,
16, 17 bottom, 18 left, 18/19 bottom, 19, 22,
23, 24, 25, 26 bottom, 27, 29; *Michael
Chinery* 7 bottom, 9 top, 10 center,
12 bottom, 13 top left & right,
14/15 bottom, 15 top; *Michael &
Patricia Fogden* 5 top, 11 top right,
13 bottom left, 18 top, 20/21, 26
top, 28; *Susan Fogden* 9 bottom
right, 17 top.

1234567890
Printed in Hong Kong by
Wing King Tong Co. Ltd 543210

❊ CONTENTS ❊

❋ RESOURCES AND CONSERVATION ❋

TROPICAL RAINFORESTS grow in the hot, wet regions close to the equator. Temperatures are high all year, and it rains nearly every day. These conditions are ideal for plants and the rainforests contain a greater variety than any other **habitat**. Although rainforests cover only about one-twentieth of the world's land surface, more than half the known plant **species** live there, and almost as many animal species. The dense mass of trees helps to maintain worldwide patterns of climate and to protect the earth from **global warming**.

PLANTS, PEOPLE, AND PRODUCTS

Plants and animals provide everything the **indigenous peoples** of the rainforests need: food, clothing, medicines, building materials, and even transport – in the form of **dug-out canoes**. The traditional way of life does not harm the forests, but outsiders who cut the trees for profit destroy large areas. Huge areas are also cleared for farmland. Scientists estimate that about 100 acres (40.5 hectares) of rainforest are lost every minute. That is the area of roughly 100 football fields.

HOPE FOR THE FORESTS

ONCE a large area of rainforest has been cut down (below left), it will not regrow. Small areas, however, can regrow. Many poor people depend on the forests for their living. If they can cut down the trees they need for their own purposes and then sell a small quantity, the forests can survive and flourish as they have done for thousands of years. The best hope is to stop large-scale logging and to turn the forests into **national parks**, like this one in Costa Rica (below right), where plants and animals – and people's livelihoods – will be protected.

About 50 species of plants and animals are lost every day as their rainforest homes and habitats are destroyed. Some of them might have been useful medicines.

Forest products, including timber, food, and rubber, are in demand all over the world, but the forests cannot meet the demand. Many valuable timber trees have become extremely rare and some are in danger of disappearing forever.

SAVING THE FORESTS

Many people and organizations are desperately trying to stop the destruction of the rainforests. Everyone in the world needs the forests, so international, national, and individual efforts are needed.

▼ People who follow traditional ways of life, do not harm the habitat. This woman from the Congo rainforest in Central Africa, is building a shelter. The indigenous peoples do not like the destruction of their land.

▲ Colorful *macaws* are still common in some parts of the Amazon rainforest, but they cannot survive if their forest homes are destroyed.

❋ TREES AND TIMBER ❋

TROPICAL RAINFORESTS contain thousands of different kinds of trees, with many different uses. It has been estimated that over 3,531 million cubic feet (100 million cubic meters) of timber is taken from the rainforests each year. Nearly three-quarters of this comes from Southeast Asia, where large areas have already completely lost their rainforests. About two-thirds of the timber removed from the rainforests and other tropical forests is burned in power stations or used to fuel cooking stoves. The rest are used all over the world in buildings and for making furniture and other objects.

SOFTWOODS AND HARDWOODS

Most of the world's timber comes from **conifer** trees that grow in cool northern forests and **plantations**. The timber grows quickly and is cheap, but it is soft and does not last as long as timbers from the flowering trees, which are called **hardwoods**.

▼ Cutting down a few trees to support small communities does not harm the forest. These woodcutters are Bambuti people from the Congo rainforest.

AFRICAN GIANT
• •

KAPOK trees are the tallest trees in Africa. Their massive trunks, supported by big buttress roots, can tower over 197 feet (60 meters) high. Kapok timber is used for **plywood**, but the tree is best known for the silky fibers that surround its seeds. The fibers are used for stuffing sleeping bags, life jackets, and toys.

TOUGH TIMBERS

• • • • • • • • • • • • • • • • • • •

Brazilian rosewood comes from the coastal rainforests of Brazil. It is one of the best woods for guitars, but it has become so rare that the remaining trees are strictly protected. People are trying to establish plantations, but it will be a long time before guitar-makers can use this timber again. Ebony and similar timbers are ideal for making musical instruments, because they produce clear tones. Many of them are now scarce. Ironwood, or ekki, which comes from West Africa, is used for canal gates, and harbor walls because it is resistant to water and insect attack. Mahogany has a deep red color. It has been used for making expensive chairs and cabinets. True mahogany trees have become rare in the rainforests of Central and South America. Even some of the poorer substitute timbers are now difficult to find. Teak is a tough timber full of water-resisting oils. It was once widely used in shipbuilding and for making floors. These teak logs (above), cut from a forest in Southeast Asia, will soon be sold.

The hardness of many tropical timbers and their resistance to decay make them valuable for building. Attractive colors and grains make many of them ideal for fine furniture, ornaments, and musical instruments.

Today, many people admire antiques made of hardwoods, but avoid buying anything new made of tropical hardwood unless they know that the wood has been grown on a plantation.

◀ Dipterocarp trees, with their yellowish leaves, are among the biggest and most important timber trees in Southeast Asia. Some of these hard, dark timbers are called Philippine mahoganies.

▶ This man in Sierra Leone in West Africa is carrying firewood home from the forest. Outside big towns, most people living in the tropics burn wood to heat their water and cook their food.

GRASS HOUSES

Bamboos are taller than many trees, but they are not trees. They are actually giant grasses with hollow, woody stems. Often called canes, these stems have many uses. Forest-dwelling people build their houses entirely of bamboo, and elsewhere in the tropics the sturdy stems are used as **scaffolding**. The poles are much lighter than steel but nearly as strong. They are also used for building bridges and as water pipes. Homes in many parts of the world also have furniture made from bamboo. Over 1,000 different products are obtained from the various kinds of bamboo.

RUBBER TREES

Rubber comes from the milky juice, called **latex**, of the rubber tree. This tree is a native of Brazil, but almost all of the world's natural rubber now comes from Southeast Asia. Although most of it is produced in big plantations, employing hundreds of people, there are numerous small plantations each owned and looked after by a single family.

The sticky latex oozes from the trees when the bark is cut and drips into little cups attached to the trees. After collection, the latex is mixed with acid in large tanks. This converts it to sticky lumps, which are rolled into sheets. When these sheets are dry, they are packed off to factories to be made into tires and other products. On small plantations, the sheets of raw rubber are dried in the open and look like laundry hanging on a line.

PLANTATIONS
• •

MANY rainforest fruits, such as bananas and pineapples, are now eaten all over the world. Some are still gathered from the natural rainforest, but there is a great demand for the fruits. Large areas of rainforest have been cut down and turned into plantations on which a single crop is grown and sold for cash.

◄ Rubber trees grow in neat lines on this plantation in Thailand.

► The process of collecting latex from a rubber tree is called tapping. Cutting the bark is a skilled job. If the cuts are too deep the tree will be injured and it will not produce regular supplies of latex.

Timber and rubber trees are also grown on plantations. Trees and fruits grown on a large scale are much easier to harvest than those growing scattered through the forest, and less forest is destroyed. Plantations can never be as rich in wildlife as the natural forests. This banana plantation in central Africa is in an area cleared of forest.

▲ A fisherman on the West African coast hollows out a tree trunk to make a slender canoe. He has chosen a tree with strong, light timber so that the canoe will be easy to lift out of the water.

LONGEST STEMS IN THE WORLD
. . . .

THIS Malaysian man is preparing fine strips of cane that will be used for binding building materials together. The cane comes from climbing palms called **rattans**. Their rope-like stems may be as long as 600 feet (183 meters), though most of them are only finger-thick.

Sharp, curved spines on the leaves cling to the trees. Rattans grow mainly in Southeast Asia. Thousands of tons/tonnes are harvested every year and used to make cane furniture. The crop provides many jobs in the harvesting and preparation of the cane, but the rattans will not survive if there are no trees for them to climb.

FOODS OF THE FOREST

THE RAINFOREST is like a gigantic supermarket, full of fruit and other foods. Because the weather stays warm throughout the year, there are flowers blooming and trees in fruit all year rather than in one season only. There is always plenty for people and wild animals to eat.

▼The Agouti, a South American rodent, listens for falling Brazil nut fruits and then dashes out to eat them. Few other animals can bite through the hard shells.

CHOCOLATE AND NUTS

Cocoa, also known as cacao, originally came from the Amazon rainforest, but now most cocoa trees are grown on vast plantations in West Africa. Cocoa trees are quite small and their fruits, which look like small footballs, grow on the trunks and branches. Inside the pods are dozens of seeds. These are the cocoa beans which are roasted and crushed to make cocoa powder and chocolate.

Brazil nuts grow on very large trees in the Amazon rainforest. The woody fruit resembles a big tennis ball and weighs up to four pounds (1.8 kg). It contains up to twenty-four hard-shelled seeds, which are the nuts that we buy and eat.

▶ The husks of cashew nuts contain an irritating poison that is made harmless by roasting. Workers avoid touching the nuts until they have been roasted.

▼ Shoppers can choose from a variety of foods at this open-air market in Southeast Asia.

Eat More Brazil Nuts

BRAZIL nuts are not grown on plantations because the trees do not produce fruit outside their natural surroundings. This is because they depend on a particular kind of bee to **pollinate** their flowers, and the bee also needs to feed on a particular kind of orchid that grows only in the forest. Brazil nut trees are protected in Brazil, but the surrounding forest is often destroyed so they still do not produce any nuts. One way to help conserve the forest is to eat more Brazil nuts! A demand for the nuts will ensure that the forest is protected. This will also help the forest people because they will get an income from harvesting the nuts (left).

▲ Bananas grow in huge bunches, weighing up to 80 pounds (36 kg). Each bunch may hold over 200 bananas. The large pink bud houses tiny, male flowers.

▲ Cocoa pods grow straight from the branch. Cocoa has been cultivated in various parts of Central and South America for more than 2,500 years. The forest peoples discovered chocolate.

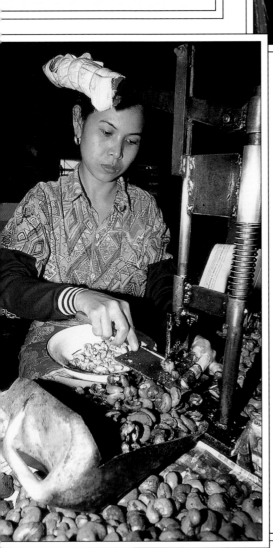

Bananas and Pineapples

Bananas are one of the most important tropical fruits. Most have a high sugar content and are a good source of energy. Some less sweet varieties, such as plantains, have a high **starch** content and are the **staple food** in many tropical areas, including central Africa.

Millions of tons/tonnes of bananas are grown on plantations every year and exported all over the world. Bananas originated in Southeast Asia, but the main growing areas are now in South and Central America and in West Africa. Although often called a tree, the banana plant is really a large herb. Its "trunk" is composed of the dead bases of its huge leaves.

The pineapple is a native of the South American rainforest, but pineapples are now grown in plantations all over the tropics. Their juicy flesh is full of sugar and **vitamins**. Hawaii and Malaysia are the main pineapple-growing regions. Millions of tons/ tonnes are harvested every year and sold as fresh or canned fruit, or made into pineapple juice.

AWFUL SMELL, SWEET TASTE

Walking under a durian tree can be smelly and dangerous. The spiky, football-sized fruits can weigh over eight pounds (3.6 kg), but they are easy to find because they smell like rotting fish. Regardless of the smell, orangutans feast on the deliciously sweet flesh. Forest people too are so keen to obtain fresh durians that they camp near the trees when the fruits begin to ripen. Wild durian trees can reach heights of about 100 feet (30.5 m), but most durian fruit are now grown on smaller trees on plantations in Southeast Asia.

COCONUT SUPERMARKET

The coconut palm has been called nature's own supermarket because it provides so many useful things. Its trunk provides fuel and timber for buildings and boats. Its leaves are used for covering roofs of houses. Its fruit, the coconut itself, has several useful layers. Young fruits contain refreshing coconut milk inside the tasty white flesh. The dried flesh of mature fruits, known as **copra**, is crushed to make coconut oil. This is mostly used to make soap and cosmetics. The residue makes good food for cattle. The tough fibers, called **coir**, that surround the coconut shell are used to make rope and coconut matting, and the shells themselves make good firewood.

Coconut palms probably originated in the coastal forests of Malaysia. Today they grow wild and are cultivated in all tropical regions. Millions of acres/hectares of rainforest have been cleared for coconut plantations.

▲ Pineapples do not grow on trees. They grow on short, spiky plants near the ground.

▼ Empty coconut husks are stored on the edge of a plantation. They will be taken to a factory where the fibers are made into ropes and mats.

Paw-Paws, Guavas, and Mangoes

PAW-PAWS (above), also called papayas, originated in the American rainforests, but are now grown on plantations in tropical areas of world. Some varieties are green, while others are yellow or orange when ripe. Guavas from tropical America and mangoes from Asia look very similar. They contain lots of vitamins and their juices are good to drink.

▲ It is a long climb to get the coconuts which grow under the crown of leaves on the coconut palm.

▼ The breadfruit is full of starch. The fruit is sliced, cooked, and eaten like bread. The trunks of breadfruit trees are used to make canoes and the bark fibers to make cloth.

▲ The avocado pear is a native of Central America, and is a favorite food of the quetzal. Wild avocados are small, but are still quite a mouthful for the 15-inch (38-cm) bird.

SUGAR AND STARCH

The rainforest supermarket does not only contain fruit. Many other parts of plants can be eaten or used to sweeten or flavor other foods. Medicines and other useful products can also be obtained from leaves and bark (see pages 18-19). All green plants make their own food by a process called **photosynthesis**, which takes place only in sunlight. During the process, the plants absorb **carbon dioxide** gas from the air and combine it with water to make sugar. Oxygen is given out at the same time. Sugar cane and some other plants store the sugar in their stems or roots, but most plants turn the sugar into starch before storing it.

Sugar cane is a large grass that stores sugar in its stems, or canes. The harvested stems are crushed to extract the sugar. Depending on the amount of processing it gets, the cane can produce both brown and white sugar. The plant's original home was around the edges of the rainforests of New Guinea and Southeast Asia, but it is now grown throughout the tropics and yields about 100 million tons/tonnes of sugar every year. This is more than half of the world's sugar supply.

Starch is full of energy, and starch-rich foods are the staple diet of people all over the world. Cereals and potatoes provide much of the starch in cooler countries, but in the tropics there is a wider range of plants rich in starch.

▲ This young girl from Ecuador is preparing a meal from chopped and cooked cassava roots.

▶ Harvesting cassava is hard work. The tubers develop at the base of cane-like stems, up to nine feet (2.7 meters) high.

◀ Sugar cane is being harvested. Most sugar plantations are on land that was once covered by rainforests. Some new farmed varieties can be grown in cooler places.

Starchy tropical plants include yams, sweet potatoes, and most important of all, cassava. All of these plants store their food in swollen roots or underground stems.

Cassava, known as manioc in South America, grows in wet tropical areas. As many as 500 million people eat it in some form or other at nearly every meal. Its swollen roots are full of starch and can be cooked and eaten like potatoes or dried and ground up to make a kind of flour. Cassava is a native of South America, but it is now grown in other tropical areas.

SAGO FLOWERS AND SAGO FLOUR

Sago palms grow in the wet forests of Southeast Asia. Each tree flowers only once in its life, when it is about 15 years old. Before then, it stores a large amount of starch in its trunk in preparation for the time when it produces its big flower bunches. Forest people, and commercial **cultivators**, cut down the trees before they are due to flower. They scrape out the starchy pith, which may weigh as much as 900 pounds (408 kg), crush it, and wash out the starch, which dries as sago flour. When trees are cut down, new ones grow from the roots.

OIL PALMS

The oil palm, which is a native of West Africa, is one of the most important sources of vegetable oil. Each year the tree produces up to six big bunches of fruit. Each fruit is rather like a plum, with a fleshy outer region surrounding a hard stone containing a seed, or **kernel**. Both the flesh and the kernel are full of oil.

Palm oil is used for making margarine, cosmetics, soap, and many other products. In some places it is even used to fuel the local taxis. There are large oil palm plantations in Africa and Southeast Asia, and good crops are taken from wild trees in West Africa.

The copaiba tree also produces oil, but here the oil is in the trunk. A single tree can produce up to ten gallons (37.9 liters) of oil each year, and it can go straight into a **diesel engine** without any refining. Copaiba plantations may one day produce enough oil to supply small towns.

SPICES

STARCHY foods provide a lot of energy, but they do not have much taste. Their flavor can be improved by adding spices from the seeds, barks, and roots of a variety of rainforest plants.
Cinnamon comes from the inner bark of a small tree that originated in the forests of Sri Lanka and southern India.
Cloves are the dried flower buds of a small tree that originally came from Indonesia, although most of the world's cloves are now grown on the islands of Zanzibar and Madagascar.
Ginger comes from the underground stems of a small bamboo-like plant that came originally from the forests of

◀ Oil palm plantations produce more oil from a given area than any other crop. The trees are grown from seeds and they start producing their oil-filled fruits when they are about five years old.

▶ Large oil palm plantations have their own processing factories.

tropical Asia. The flowers spring from a cone-like structure (below left).

Nutmeg is the seed of an Indonesian tree. The dark seed is visible inside this opened fruit (above). The red network around the seed provides another spice called mace.

Pepper comes from the fruits of a climbing plant that originally grew in Southeast Asia. Unripe fruits are dried to produce black peppercorns, while white pepper is obtained by crushing the seeds of ripe fruits after removing the skin.

Vanilla is obtained from the seed pods of an orchid. The plant originated in Mexico, but is now cultivated in several other tropical areas.

The spice, usually sold as a vanilla essence, is taken from the dried pods. Vanilla is the most expensive of the tropical spices.

▲ A woman is treading the sago pith on a rattan mat, before washing out the starch. Sago flour is a staple food for the nomadic Penan people of Borneo.

FOREST PHARMACY

NEARLY 7,000 plant species growing in the forests of Southeast Asia are known to have some **medicinal** value, and the people of the Amazon use over 1,300 different kinds of plants as cures. Indigenous people know the secrets of nearly all the plants around them and exactly which kind of bark or leaf to use for each illness.

Doctors and scientists have proven how important these plants are for curing diseases. About one-quarter of all the medicines and other **pharmaceutical** products that we buy today probably came from some type of rainforest plant. Rainforests have been described as giant pharmacies containing useful medicines.

PRECIOUS POISONS

SEVERAL indigenous rainforest peoples hunt with poison darts or arrows. In South America the poison usually comes from arrow-poison frogs (above), whose skins contain some of the most deadly of all poisons. Some arrow poisons, including curare, come from plants. Curare is obtained by crushing the bark of various plants. It is normally deadly, but surgeons use it in tiny doses to relax muscles and make surgery easier.

▼ Rainforest people in several parts of the world fish with the use of poisonous plants. Bundles of plants are placed in a stream and the poison seeps out to infect any fish swimming in the surrounding water.

▶ A hunter from the Amazon rainforest sharpens the tip of a poison dart to ensure that it will remain embedded in the flesh of his prey.

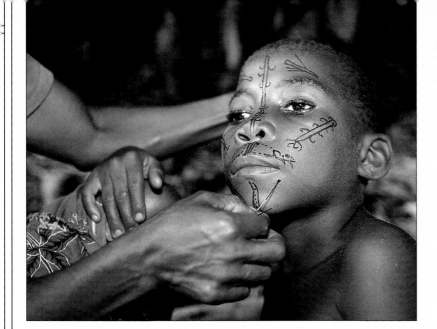

BARK is full of chemicals, many of which protect the trees from insect attack. Some also have important medical uses. Quinine, which is an important medicine for fighting **malaria**, comes from the bark of the South American cinchona tree. African Pygmies get nearly all their medicines from trees and climbers, and about three-quarters of them come from bark or sap. Plant dyes and juices are also used for decoration. This Pygmy girl (left) is having her face painted with a mixture of charcoal and plant sap.

A visit to the dentist may well involve one or more rainforest products. Before filling a cavity, the drilled surface of the tooth is usually treated with a **resin** from the oil-producing South American copaiba tree. If you need a root filling, it will probably be made of gutta-percha – a rubbery substance obtained from trees growing in Southeast Asia. Once the chemical makeup of the medicines has been identified, it is possible for pharmaceutical companies to produce some of them artificially, but many drugs are still made with natural plant substances.

PAINKILLERS AND GERM-KILLERS

Rainforest plants provide us with painkillers, **anesthetics**, cough remedies, muscle relaxants, drugs to speed up or slow down the heart, and numerous germ-killers. Several drugs used for treating cancer also come from rainforest plants, and some have even been found in butterflies. Scientists have so far studied only a small proportion of rainforest plants, although many more useful medicines may yet be discovered. This is one very good reason for conserving the living laboratory of the rainforests.

PRECIOUS PERIWINKLE

THE rosy periwinkle, originally from the forests of Madagascar, now grows like a weed in many tropical areas. But it is a very useful weed: chemicals extracted from the leaves have been successful in treating leukemia and some other forms of cancer. Unfortunately, the medicines are expensive because it takes 53 tons/tonnes of leaves to produce 3.5 ounces (100 grams) of one of the drugs.

❋ RAINFORESTS AND CLIMATE ❋

RAINFORESTS HELP to keep the world's climate patterns more or less stable. Destruction of the forests, especially the huge Amazon forest, would cause climatic changes all over the world.

FLOODS AND DROUGHTS

Most of the rain falling on the forest is quickly soaked up by the trees. The leaves pump it back into the air in the form of water vapor, and then it condenses and produces more rain. Loss of the forest would immediately make the local climate much drier. There would still be some rain, but with no trees to soak it up, it would wash the soil into the rivers and the swollen rivers would cause severe floods. This already happens in some parts of the world.

The forests also affect the amount of heat in the atmosphere by means of what is called the mirror effect (see panel). Destruction of the forests would overheat the atmosphere. This would change the air circulation and alter the climate all over the world. There would be less rain close to the **equator**, and more rain in the Caribbean and in parts of the Sahara Desert in Africa. But Europe and North America would become much drier, with serious droughts and crop failures.

GLOBAL WARMING

Every year the rainforests soak up millions of tons/ tonnes of carbon dioxide from the atmosphere. Much of this comes from burning oil and coal, and from burning forests. Scientists have shown that, because of the greenhouse effect (see panel), an increase in the amount of carbon dioxide in the air can lead to global warming, a rise in the average temperature of the whole planet.

Rising temperatures will cause the polar ice caps to melt and the sea level to rise. As a result, many lands will disappear under the sea. Protecting the remaining rainforests will help to delay the problem and increasing them will slow it down even further. But the real solution to global warming is to cut down the amount of carbon dioxide that we pump into the air, by reducing the amount of fuel we burn.

▶ The dense, dark green vegetation of the rainforest absorbs light, heat, and carbon dioxide. It creates rain and releases oxygen, helping the world to breathe.

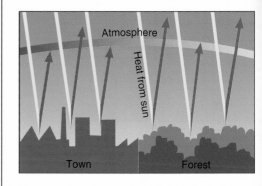

GREENHOUSE EFFECT

THE earth's atmosphere acts like a greenhouse, holding a layer of warm air near the surface but releasing some heat back into space. When there is too much carbon dioxide, extra heat is trapped. Without vegetation to absorb the carbon dioxide, dangerous levels build up and global warming occurs.

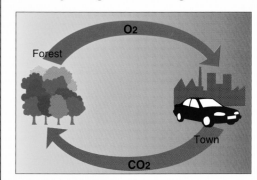

CARBON CYCLE

PLANTS take in carbon dioxide (CO_2) and give off the oxygen (O_2) that we breathe. A few years ago it was estimated that nearly 350 billion tons/tonnes of carbon was locked in the rainforest trees. If the forests are destroyed, large amounts of carbon dioxide will be released into the air because there will be no more plants to soak it up. The amount of CO_2 in the air is already increasing. One hundred and fifty years ago carbon dioxide made up 0.029 percent of the atmosphere, but today the figure is closer to 0.035 percent, and it is going up every year.

Rain falls

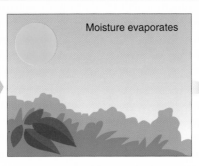
Moisture evaporates

Clouds form

WATER CYCLE

RAIN falling every day helps plants grow. Rainforest trees and other plants soak up most of the rain falling on them. They use some of it to make food. The rest evaporates from the leaves and returns to the atmosphere as water vapor. This vapor condenses to form more clouds, which produce more rain. If there is a loss in the number of trees, the cycle is broken. The results would be less water vapor returning to the atmosphere and the climate becoming drier.

MIRROR EFFECT

RAINFORESTS absorb about 85 percent of the sun's heat falling on them and reflect the other 15 percent back into the atmosphere. Farmland reflects about 20 percent of the sun's heat, while the earth and built-up areas reflect about 30 percent.

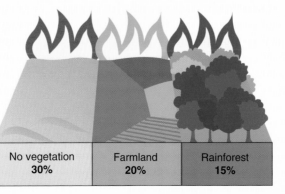

| No vegetation 30% | Farmland 20% | Rainforest 15% |

❂ FOREST CLEARANCE ❂

TODAY, RAINFORESTS are under attack on a massive scale and are disappearing at a fast rate. The **United Nations** recently announced that nearly 34.6 million acres (14 million hectares) of rainforest are being burned or cut down every year. Fifty years ago about 15 percent of the world's land surface was covered with rainforest. Today, the figure is under seven percent. In 50 years, more than half of the rainforest has disappeared, along with unknown numbers of forest animals.

CROPS AND CATTLE

Most of the cleared forest land is used for large-scale growing of crops, such as **maize**, or for rearing cattle. But the soils are usually poor and cannot produce good crops for more than a few years. Pastures also become worn out through over-grazing. The land becomes useless. It takes a long time for the forest to grow back because there are no trees nearby to produce the necessary seeds. It might not return to forest at all because, once the trees have gone, there might not be enough rain or soil (see page 20).

DEADLY FIRES

FIRE often occurs naturally in forests, as a result of lightning or volcanic eruptions (above). But fire is also regularly used by cultivators to clear forest land before planting crops. The fires sometimes get out of hand and spread to other areas of the rainforest, especially in those areas that experience a dry season. If the rains are late, the fires continue to burn and cause severe damage. This happened in Indonesia in 1997. Smoke from numerous fires blocked out the sun for hundreds of miles and caused many problems in neighboring countries. Parts of the Brazilian rainforest have also been badly damaged by fires.

RENEWABLE TIMBER SUPPLIES

. . . .

RAINFOREST trees have long been cut down for building and for making furniture, and until recently no one thought about replacing the trees. The International Tropical Timber Organization, with support from over 100 countries, is now working to ensure that the forests are managed properly and that all trees cut for timber are replaced with young ones. Timber from protected species cannot be exported without documents showing that it has come from a renewable resource. This helps to conserve those rainforest areas with valuable timber trees, but it will not help areas like this one (above) where the trees have been cleared to make way for agriculture.

DESTRUCTION FOR INDUSTRY

Tropical forests provide large amounts of firewood for power stations and domestic stoves. Any type of tree can be used for this. Large areas of forest are also destroyed every year to provide timber for the chemical industry. Wood is shredded or chipped, and then treated with chemicals to produce **cellulose**, rayon, and other fibers.

Many rainforests are sitting on vast oil and mineral deposits. Brazil, for example, has a large amount of iron deposits. Mining of minerals and drilling for oil have already destroyed large areas of rainforest and poisoned the surrounding soil and rivers with waste materials. Other areas of forest have been cut to provide the fuel needed for processing the minerals.

Elsewhere, large areas of rainforest have been converted into plantations of rubber trees, oil palms, and fruit trees. The land still has trees, but the variety of plant life is lost, along with all the animal life that depended on it.

◀ Small patches of forest are cleared by villagers to plant vegetable gardens, but it quickly grows back when the people move on to a new area.

▶ Another truck load of logs pulls out of the forest. One man with a chain saw can cut down several giant trees in a day. Some of the trees may have taken a thousand years to grow.

❈ RESCUING THE RAINFORESTS ❈

PEOPLE HAVE lived in rainforests for thousands of years without doing any harm to the environment. Cutting a few trees for timber, or to make room for small gardens was no more damaging than the natural death of old trees, because new trees soon took their place and filled in the clearings when the people moved on. The forest animals were also unaffected. But no plant or animal can survive if its habitat is destroyed.

TIGER HUNTERS

ONE hundred years ago there were over 100,000 tigers in the world. Today there are only about 5,000. They are in danger because their forest habitat is disappearing, and also because they are hunted. Tiger skins bring in a lot of money, and their bones are also in demand for use in Chinese medicine. Very few tigers are left in the rainforests of Southeast Asia. This one (below) is safe in a reserve.

▲ The orangutan is in danger of losing its forest home in Southeast Asia because of forest clearing. It is also in demand for the pet trade. Hunters will often capture the young apes so that they can sell them.

ENDANGERED SPECIES

Many rainforest plants and animals are now facing **extinction** because they are losing their homes. About 1,000 of the world's tree species are believed to be in danger, and most of these are in rainforests. Every day, unknown numbers of plant and animal species disappear as their homes are burned or destroyed. When they have gone they can never come back.

Indigenous rainforest peoples traditionally hunt for food, but this is rarely a problem. If the animals become scarce the people usually move to another area. Organized hunting to make money is a different matter. Many macaws and other parrots are now endangered because so many have been caught for the pet trade. Ocelots and other spotted wildcats have been killed for their beautiful coats. Food markets openly sell the flesh of chimpanzees and other animals as "bush meat".

Many conservation organizations are trying hard to prevent the extinction of more animals. These organizations buy land for reserves and pay wardens to guard them against **poachers**.

GORILLA VICTIMS

THE mountain gorilla (above) lives in the mountain forests of Central Africa, where it was threatened with extinction by a recent war. The animals were killed by landmines and shot by soldiers, and a large area of their forest home was cut down to provide farmland for the people escaping the war.
Only about 630 gorillas survived the war, but their numbers are slowly increasing now that the fighting has decreased. The national parks in the area have re-opened, and grants from conservation organizations enable them to be patrolled regularly. Without the patrols, the animals would be at risk from poachers looking for trophies and meat to sell.

CONSERVING THE FORESTS

The conservationist's first aim is to protect the habitat by creating nature reserves or national parks, where wildlife is managed and protected. In rainforest areas, this usually means doing nothing more than keeping poachers out. Less than ten percent of all rainforests are protected in this way.

NATURE RESERVES

Nature reserves are often very small. They are sometimes owned by local organizations and they are usually set up to conserve a special habitat or in some cases one particular kind of animal. National parks are generally much bigger than nature reserves. They are usually set up to protect whole regions and their wildlife, and they often cover several different habitats.

▲ Footpaths and suspension bridges have been built to make walking through the forests easier for tourists. Conservationists have to make sure that the wildlife is not disturbed or that the landscape is not damaged.

▼ Safe in the arms of a *ranger*, this young chimp was taken from the wild before it could be captured and sold. The poachers shot the mother and sold her as bush meat.

POVERTY AND TRADE

· · · · · · · · · · · · · · · · · · ·

THE people who live in rainforest areas are often poor. It is unfair to expect them to conserve wild animals when they do not have enough food to feed their families. There is a demand for the skins and body parts of wild animals to be used as trophies and jungle remedies. The local people meet the demand, even though the cures may not be real. If the rainforest animals are to be saved, then people from richer countries must help the people from poorer countries to save them. Most of the world's countries have signed up to CITES – the Convention on International Trade in Endangered Species – which controls all commercial trade in endangered plants and animals. Licences are necessary for importing and exporting the endangered species, whether they are alive or dead. It is almost impossible to sell the most endangered species, and if there is no market for them, hunting will not be worthwhile.

▶ The golden lion tamarin almost disappeared when most of its forest home in Brazil was destroyed. Captive breeding has ensured its survival, and one day it might be possible to put some of the animals back into the wild – as long as there is enough forest for them to live in.

NATIONAL PARKS

Most countries with areas of rainforest have established national parks to protect at least some of the forest. Costa Rica, in Central America, is one of the most conservation-minded countries, with national parks and other reserves covering almost 30 percent of the land. Most of the protected land is rainforest.

▼ Tourism is big business for national parks, many of which have comfortable lodges for visitors to stay in. Local people earn money looking after the tourists and this encourages them to conserve the rainforests.

RARE BEAUTIES

AS some species become rare, their commercial value increases. There is a big demand for tropical plants, especially orchids (above), in the **horticultural** trade and many species have become rare. Queen Alexandra's birdwing, one of the world's rarest butterflies, is in danger of losing its habitat to the oil palm plantations spreading rapidly through the African country of New Guinea. It is strictly protected but its huge size, combined with its rarity, makes it attractive to collectors.

HAVENS FOR WILDLIFE

KORUP National Park in Cameroon, West Africa, was established in 1986 to protect about 300,000 acres (121,400 hectares) of the oldest and richest rainforest habitat in Africa. The area has never been disturbed and it contains over 400 different kinds of trees. There are also many rare birds and monkeys, including the endangered **drill**. The rivers contain about 150 different kinds of fish. The central area of the park is strictly protected and only a few tourists and scientists are allowed to visit it. **Biologists** studying this region are discovering dozens of new animals and plants every year.

Khao Yai National Park in the center of Thailand covers an area of almost 500,000 acres (202,350 hectares). Most of this is rainforest, sheltering gibbons, tigers, elephants, and over 2,000 different kinds of flowering plants, including a wonderful array of orchids.

Costa Rica's national parks are a shining example to the world. They cover almost one fifth of the whole country and attract naturalists, tourists, and filmmakers. These children (left) are enjoying a walk along the forest trail in the Monteverde Cloud Forest Reserve in Costa Rica. This famous nature reserve, owned and managed by the Tropical Science Center of San José, is very wet, but it has an excellent network of trails from which visitors can see a variety of butterflies, hummingbirds, and many other animals.

◄ Aerial walkways constructed high in the trees allow visitors to get close enough to photograph the exotic flowers, birds, and other animals that never come down to the ground.

▲ This baby orangutan is being fed at a feeding station in Borneo. One day, it could be returned to freedom.

It shelters about 1,000 different kinds of butterflies and 800 species of birds, including the beautiful quetzal (see page 13).

National parks are not created entirely for wildlife conservation. People continue to live there and may farm some of the outer areas. Tourism is important and many parks are regularly visited by groups of **naturalists** from all over the world. The money the visitors pay, goes towards the maintenance of the park.

Local people work as park guides and rangers. They know a lot about the forest wildlife and they show visitors around as well as doing essential work, such as maintaining footpaths. The people might originally have lived by hunting or cutting wood in the forests, but they are now paid to protect the trees and wildlife.

☀ GLOSSARY ☀

Anesthetic Any substance used to bring about unconsciousness or local loss of feeling.

Biologist A scientist who studies living things.

Carbohydrate Any kind of food material consisting of carbon, hydrogen, and oxygen. Starch and sugar are good examples. Carbohydrates provide energy.

Carbon cycle The circulation of carbon-containing material, especially carbon dioxide gas, between living things and their surroundings. Animals give out carbon dioxide and plants absorb it to make food, so the amount in the atmosphere stays more or less constant.

Carbon dioxide A gas in the atmosphere that plants use for photosynthesis.

Cellulose The main substance of the cell walls of plants and of wood.

Coir The fibrous material that makes up the outer layer of the coconut fruit.

Conifer Any plant that carries its pollen and seeds in cones. Most conifers are large trees and most of them are evergreen.

Conservation The scientific management of a natural habitat, such as a rainforest, designed to ensure the survival of the maximum possible numbers of plant and animal species.

Copra The dried flesh of coconuts.

Dug-out canoe A canoe made by hollowing out a single tree trunk.

Endangered species Any species that is in danger of extinction (see below).

Equator The imaginary line around the center of the earth, midway between the north and south poles.

Extinction The total disappearance of a particular plant or animal species from the earth.

Global warming Worldwide increase in temperatures, believed to result from increasing amounts of carbon dioxide in the atmosphere.

Greenhouse effect The way in which the atmosphere, acting like the glass in a greenhouse, traps the sun's heat and keeps the earth warm.

▲ A rainforest has layers of vegetation. Low shrubs grow on the forest floor, and slender young trees form an understorey below the vast, dense canopy of tree-tops. At intervals taller trees called emergents poke their heads through the canopy. All the plants are trying to get a share of the sunlight.

Habitat The natural home of a plant or animal species. It may be a whole forest or just a tree trunk, or even a pool of water trapped by a plant.

Hardwood Timber obtained from flowering trees as opposed to cone-bearing trees.

Kernel The seed inside a nut.

Latex The milky and often rather sticky fluid in certain plants, such as the rubber tree.

Malaria A serious disease carried by certain mosquitoes, especially in tropical areas.

Medicinal Something that can heal.

National Park An area where development is strictly controlled, so that the scenery and wildlife remain to be enjoyed by everyone.

Naturalist A scientist who studies plants and animals in their natural surroundings.

Photosynthesis The process by which green plants make food. The plants use energy from sunlight to convert water and carbon dioxide gas into sugar.

ENDANGERED!

RAINFORESTS are vitally important to the well-being of the world but they are in danger of destruction. Many of the animals and plants featured in this book are under threat from forest clearance. If you are interested in knowing more about rainforests and in helping to conserve them, you may find these addresses and websites useful.

Friends of the Earth, Rainforest Campaign, *26-28 Underwood Street, London N1 7JQ*

Rainforest Foundation, *A5 City Cloisters, 188-96 Old St, London EC1V 9FR*

Worldwide Fund for Nature
WWF (Australia), *Level 5, 725 George Street, Sydney, NSW 2000*
WWF (South Africa), *116 Dorp Street, Stellenbosch 7600*
WWF (UK), *Panda House, Weyside Park, Cattershall Lane, Godalming, Surrey GU17 1XR*

Worldwide Fund for Nature
http://www.wwf-uk.org

Friends of the Earth
http://www.foe.co.uk

Environmental Education Network
http://envirolink.org.enviroed/

Rainforest Foundation
http://rainforestfoundationuk.org

Rainforest Preservation Foundation
http://www.flash.net/~rpf/

Survival International
http://www.survival.org.uk

Sustainable Development
http://iisd1.iisd.ca/

Rainforest Action Network
http://www.igc.apc.org/ran/intro.html

◀ **The map shows the location of the world's main rainforest areas.**

NORTH AMERICA · EUROPE · ASIA · AFRICA · SOUTH AMERICA · AUSTRALIA · Tropic of Cancer · Equator · Tropic of Capricorn

Plantation An area that has been cleared and planted with cash crops, especially trees or shrubs. Rubber trees, oil palms, tea bushes, and bananas are all grown on plantations.

Plywood Strong, thin board consisting of layers glued together with the grains running crosswise.

Rattan One of a number of climbing palms whose flexible stems are widely used for building shelters in the rainforest and for making cane furniture.

Ranger A person who works in a national park or other reserve, looking after the wildlife and guiding tourists.

Resin A sticky, strong-smelling substance that oozes from the bark and wood of many trees.

Softwood Timber obtained from cone-bearing trees (conifers) as opposed to flowering trees.

Species One particular kind of plant or animal, such as a teak tree or a tiger.

Staple food The main food of a population, eaten nearly every day.

Starch A form of carbohydrate stored by plants, especially in cassava, potatoes, yams, and many other root crops.

Sterile Unable to produce seeds.

Sugar Substance made by plants during photosynthesis. It is a carbohydrate that supplies humans with energy. Plants including sugar cane and sugar beet are especially rich in sugar.

Tropical Describes the tropics; areas of the world, on each side of the equator, where the climate is hot throughout the year.

Vitamins Chemical substances found in various foods that are essential for human health.

Water cycle The continuous circulation of water through the soil, rivers, seas, atmosphere, and living things.

● INDEX ●

Page numbers in *italics* refer to illustrations.